The Leaping Lions

Written by Lee Wang

Illustrated by Lachlan Creagh

Flying Start
to Literacy®

Contents

Chapter 1: The lazy lions

The Leaping Lions liked to play soccer.

They could leap high and run fast,
but they were very lazy.

They did not train to get fit
and they did not play as a team.

Their coach tried to show them what to do to play well, but they just puffed out their chests and did what they liked.

On the day they played against the Pouncing Panthers, the Leaping Lions did not play well.

They all chased the ball at the same time. They fell over each other and got in each other's way. When they got the ball, they did not pass it.

They did not play as a team.

Chapter 2: Team panther

The Pouncing Panthers played as a team.

They passed the ball from one player to another. They kicked the ball to each other. They knocked the ball to each other with their heads.

The Pouncing Panthers had the ball at their end of the soccer ground all the time and they kicked two goals.

The Leaping Lions were angry because they could not get any goals. They bumped into the Pouncing Panthers and tripped them up as they ran with the ball.

The referee blew the whistle to stop the game. He gave the Pouncing Panthers a free kick. This made the Leaping Lions angrier.

Chapter 3: Time out!

The coach of the Leaping Lions called, "Time out!"

He said to the Leaping Lions, "You are not working together. You need to play as a team."

The Leaping Lions proudly puffed out their chests. But they did not listen and they did not play as a team.

The Pouncing Panthers won the soccer game by six goals.

After the game, the Pouncing Panthers shook hands with the Leaping Lions.

The Pouncing Panthers were happy as they ran around the ground. Their fans clapped and cheered, and the team went off to a pizza party to celebrate their win.

The Leaping Lions' coach told all the lions to sit down.

He said to them, "You did not play as a team, so there will be no pizza for you tonight."

The Leaping Lions felt ashamed that they had been so lazy and so proud.

Chapter 4: The lions learn a lesson

The Leaping Lions knew it was time to change the way they played.

They decided to train hard.

They did sit-ups and stretched to reach their toes.

They did push-ups until they couldn't do any more.

They did high knee jumps and leaped
over each other.　They went on
long runs.

18

Then they crawled home together and collapsed into a big pile.

They slept and slept and slept.

Chapter 5: The new, improved lions

The next time the Leaping Lions played the Pouncing Panthers, they played as a team. They ran fast and passed the ball to each other. They kicked four goals.

The Leaping Lions defended their goal so well that the Pouncing Panthers only got one goal. The fans cheered and shouted with joy.

The Pouncing Panthers were amazed that the Leaping Lions had won the game.

The Leaping Lions were so happy.
They had played as a team and
they had won the game.

They made a big circle and they
cheered and shouted to celebrate
their win.

Then they had pizza!

A note from the author

Sometimes when I watch people play sport, I feel sad that everyone thinks that winning is more important than anything else. I think working as a team is also important, not only on the field when playing sport, but in classrooms too.

I wrote this story to show how teamwork is better than trying to win individually, and that listening to advice can help us to make better decisions.